TABLE OF CONTENTS

PHONICS

Initial Consonants	2
Short **a**	3
Short **e**	4
Short **i**	5
Short **o**	6
Short **u**	7
Short Vowel Puzzle	8
Short Vowel Review	9
Long **a**	10
Long **e**	11
Long **i**	12
Long **o**	13
Long **u**	14
Long Vowel Puzzle	15
Long Vowel Review	16

LANGUAGE ARTS

Story Order	17
Telling Sentences	18
Asking Sentences	19
Naming Words	20–21
Naming More Than One	22
Action Words	23
Adding "**s**" to Action Words	24
Describing Words	25–26
Contractions	27

MATHEMATICS

Addition	
Subtraction	
Addition and Subtraction	32, 37–38
Counting On	33
Counting Back	34
Addition Using a Number Line	35
Subtraction Using a Number Line	36
Plane Figures	39
Space Figures	40
Same Size and Shape	41
Counting by Tens	42
Tens and Ones	43–44
Greater Than and Less Than	45
Before, Between, and After	46
Pennies, Nickels, and Dimes	47–48
Time: Hours	49
Time: Half Hours	50
Time: Quarter Past the Hour	51
Time: Quarter to the Hour	52
Equal Parts of Wholes	53
Halves, Thirds, and Fourths	54
Parts of Groups	55
Picture Graph	56
Adding Three Addends	57
Adding Tens and Ones	58
Subtracting Tens and Ones	59
Addition and Subtraction Review	60

AND MORE...

Answer Key	61–63
Certificate	64

Write the first letter of each picture's name.
Read the animal names.
Write the problem numbers in the circles by the correct animals.

1. _____ _____ _____

2. _____ _____ _____

3. _____ _____ _____ _____

4. _____ _____ _____ _____

Circle the pictures whose names have the **short a** sound.

short **a** sound
hat

1.

2.

3.

4.

Circle the pictures whose names have the **short e** sound.

short e sound
shell

 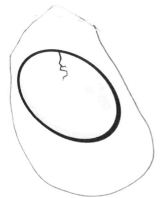  

1.

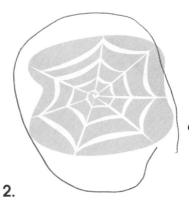  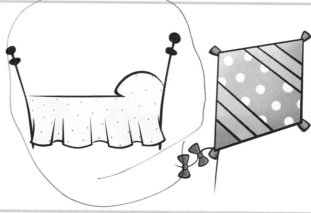

2.

3.

4.

SHORT I

Circle the pictures whose names have the **short i** sound.

1.

2.

3.

4.

Circle the pictures whose names have the **short o** sound.

1.

2.

3.

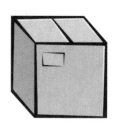   

4.

Circle the pictures whose names have the **short u** sound.

short u sound
drum

1.

   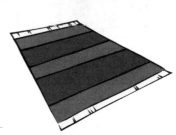

2.

3.

 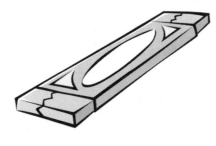  

4.

The letters **a**, **e**, **i**, **o**, and **u** are **vowels**.
These words have **short vowel** sounds:

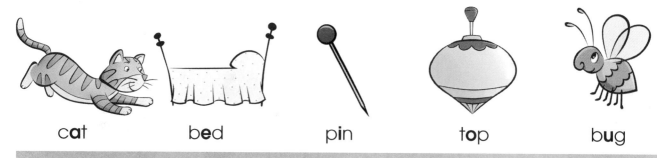

cat   bed   pin   top   bug

Look at the pictures. Say the words.
Write the short vowels in the puzzle.

ACROSS

2.

3.

5.

DOWN

1.

2.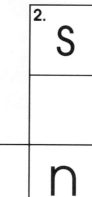

4.

	1. h		2. s		c	k
	3. t	4.		n		
		g				
5. p		g				

Write short vowels to complete the words.

a e i o u
fox

1. t__n

2. c__t

3. p__g

4. b__s

5. d__ll

6. f__n

7. f__sh

8. n__st

9. d__ck

Write the **long a** words to answer the riddles.

long a sound
snake

| rain | gray | cake |
| day | gate | snail |

1. I live in a shell.

_____

2. I wear candles on your birthday.

_____

3. I make flowers grow.

_____

4. I am the opposite of night.

_____

5. Write two **long a** words that begin with **g**.

_____ _____

_____ _____

Write the **long e** words to answer the riddles.

long **e** sound
seal

sheep	leaf	he
three	tree	me

1. I come after two.

_____

2. I grow outside.

_____

3. I say "baa!"

_____

4. I grow on a tree.

_____

5. Write two two-letter **long e** words.

_____   _____

_____   _____

Write the **long i** words to answer the riddles.

long **i** sound
kite

ice	right	tie
bike	tight	nine

1. You can ride me.

_____

2. I come before ten.

_____

3. I am very cold.

_____

4. This is the opposite of left.

_____

5. Write two **long i** words that begin with **t**.

_____ _____

_____ _____

Write the **long o** words to answer the riddles.

long o sound
coat

rose	goat	rope
nose	boat	note

1. I live on a farm.

_____

2. You can tie things with me.

_____

3. I move in water.

_____

4. I am a kind of flower.

_____

5. Write two **long o** words that begin with **n**.

_____ _____

_____ _____

Write the **long u** words to answer the riddles.

long u sound
cube

cute	tube	new
huge	few	glue

1. Toothpaste comes in a _____ .

2. Use me to stick
things together. _____

3. A whale is _____ .

4. Babies are _____ .

5. Write two **long u** words that end with **ew**.

_____   _____

_____

LONG VOWEL PUZZLE

As you've learned, the letters **a**, **e**, **i**, **o**, and **u** are **vowels**.
A **long vowel** says its own name.
These words have **long vowel** sounds:

cake

tr**ee**

hive

r**o**pe

mule

Look at the pictures. Say the words.
Write the long vowels in the puzzle.

ACROSS

1.

4.

6.

DOWN

2.

3.

5.

1. r		2. k	e		3. b
		4. t		5. b	e
		e			
				n	
6. s	l		d	e	

Draw lines from the pictures to the long vowel sounds heard in their names.

long a

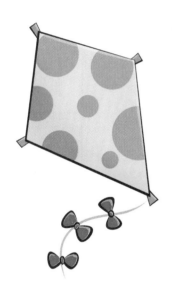

long e

long i

long o

long u

STORY ORDER

Number the pictures from 1 to 6 to show the correct order.

A **telling sentence** begins with a capital letter.
It ends with a period (**.**).

Use the ☰ to show where capital letters go.
Then put a period (**.**) at the end of each sentence.
The first one is done for you.

1. o̲ur dog is hungry.
   ☰

2. dad brings food

3. skip eats quickly

4. food goes on the floor

5. dogs are messy

6. now I need to clean up

7. Write a telling sentence.

_____

_____

_____

ASKING SENTENCES

An **asking sentence** asks about something or someone.
It ends with a question mark (**?**).

Use the ☰ to show where capital letters go. Then put a question mark (**?**)
at the end of each sentence that asks a question and a period (.) at the
end of the telling sentence. The first one is done for you.

1. <u>i</u>s Mother home**?**

2. where did she go

3. when will she be back

4. who baked the cookies

5. they are good

6. may I have another one

7. Write an asking sentence.

_____

_____

_____

_____

Some **naming words** name people or animals.

Here are a few examples:
girl   brother   cat   horse

Read the sentences. Write the naming words that name people or animals. The first one is done for you.

1. Dad drove away.

2. The farmer waved.

3. The cow was eating.

4. Our dog barked.

5. A chicken ran away.

NAMING WORDS

Some **naming words** name places or things.

Here are a few examples:

school   city   shoe   apple

Which words name places, and which words name things?
Write the words from the box on the correct lists.

zoo   house   pizza
book   town   bike

Places

Things

Write a naming word for a place and a naming word for a thing.

Place

Thing

NAMING MORE THAN ONE

Many words add **s** to name **more than one**.

Here are a few examples:
hens   frogs   rings

Add **s** to the naming words from the box to finish the sentences. The first one is done for you.

1. Jamie has two dogs.

2. One dog has brown _____.

3. One dog has black _____.

4. They run after _____.

5. They bury _____.

An **action word** tells what someone or something does.

Here are a few examples:
        jump   cry   eat   push

Read the sentences. Write the action words.
The first one is done for you.

1. Let's play ball. _____

2. Jake hits the ball. _____

3. The ball flies high. _____

4. Megan runs after it. _____

5. Will she catch it? _____

Add **s** to the action words from the box to finish the sentences.
The first one is done for you.

> plant   eat   water
> pull   grow

1. Each spring, Bob **plants** a garden.

2. He _____ pretty flowers.

3. Dad _____ weeds.

4. Anna _____ the garden.

5. Sometimes a rabbit _____ the flowers.

DESCRIBING WORDS

Some **describing words** tell how things sound or feel.

Here are a few examples:
quiet   warm   smooth

Write the describing words from the box to finish the sentences. The first one is done for you.

1. The sun is ___hot___.

2. A jet makes a _____ sound.

3. Ice cream is _____ .

4. The kitten has _____ fur.

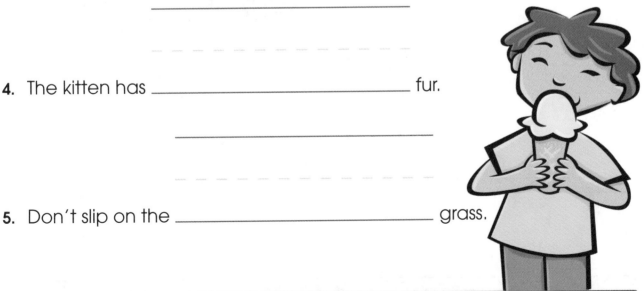

5. Don't slip on the _____ grass.

DESCRIBING WORDS

Some **describing words** tell size, color, number, or amount.

Here are a few examples:
    small   **red**   **seven**

Underline the describing words in the sentences.
The first one is done for you.

1. Lady is a <u>big</u> cat.

2. She has three kittens.

3. Tiger is the striped kitten.

4. Jet is the black kitten.

5. The little kitten is Socks.

6. We now have four cats.

7. Write a sentence using a describing word.
   Underline the describing word.

CONTRACTIONS

A **contraction** is a short way to write two words.

I am → I'm

Write the contractions for the underlined words.
The first one is done for you.

1. Please <u>do not</u> go. ___don't___

2. We <u>are not</u> done. _____

3. We <u>have not</u> painted it. _____

4. <u>Let us</u> paint it red. _____

5. It <u>will not</u> take long. _____

$2 + 1 = \underline{\ 3\ }$ $3 + 2 = \underline{\ 5\ }$

Add.

1. $3 + 1 = \underline{\quad}$

2. $1 + 1 = \underline{\quad}$

3. $2 + 2 = \underline{\quad}$

4. $1 + 3 = \underline{\quad}$

5. $3 + 2 = \underline{\quad}$

6. $2 + 1 = \underline{\quad}$

4 − 1 = __3__   5 − 2 = __3__

Subtract. Cross out pictures to show the equation.
Write how many are left.

1. 3 − 1 = ____

2. 4 − 2 = ____

3. 5 − 2 = ____

4. 4 − 3 = ____

5. 3 − 2 = ____

6. 5 − 3 = ____

$3 + 4 = \underline{\ 7\ }$

$2 + 0 = \underline{\ 2\ }$

Add.

1. $0 + 5 = \underline{\hspace{1cm}}$

2. $3 + 2 = \underline{\hspace{1cm}}$

3. $7 + 1 = \underline{\hspace{1cm}}$

4. $4 + 3 = \underline{\hspace{1cm}}$

5. $5 + 3 = \underline{\hspace{1cm}}$

6. $5 + 2 = \underline{\hspace{1cm}}$

7. $1 + 6 = \underline{\hspace{1cm}}$

8. $8 + 0 = \underline{\hspace{1cm}}$

9. $3 + 5 = \underline{\hspace{1cm}}$

10. $4 + 1 = \underline{\hspace{1cm}}$

11. $2 + 2 = \underline{\hspace{1cm}}$

12. $1 + 3 = \underline{\hspace{1cm}}$

$5 - 3 = \underline{2}$

$3 - 0 = \underline{3}$

Subtract.

1. $4 - 3 = \underline{}$ 2. $8 - 4 = \underline{}$ 3. $6 - 4 = \underline{}$

4. $6 - 5 = \underline{}$ 5. $5 - 1 = \underline{}$ 6. $8 - 6 = \underline{}$

7. $7 - 0 = \underline{}$ 8. $3 - 2 = \underline{}$ 9. $7 - 5 = \underline{}$

10. $6 - 6 = \underline{}$ 11. $7 - 1 = \underline{}$ 12. $6 - 2 = \underline{}$

The answer to an addition problem is called the **sum**.
The answer to a subtraction problem is called the **difference**.

Add to find the sum.

| 1. | 4
 + 3 | 2. | 2
 + 6 | 3. | 1
 + 7 | 4. | 2
 + 4 |

| 5. | 5
 + 2 | 6. | 5
 + 3 | 7. | 6
 + 1 | 8. | 3
 + 3 |

Subtract to find the difference.

| 9. | 6
 − 5 | 10. | 8
 − 8 | 11. | 8
 − 2 | 12. | 4
 − 2 |

| 13. | 6
 − 3 | 14. | 8
 − 6 | 15. | 7
 − 5 | 16. | 7
 − 4 |

Counting on helps you find the sum.
To count on, start with the greater number.
Count 3 more numbers than 5. The sum is 8.

$$\begin{array}{r} 5 \\ + \ 3 \\ \hline 8 \end{array}$$

6, 7, 8

0 1 2 3 4 5 6 7 8 9 10 11 12

Count on to find the sum.

1. $4 + 8 =$ _____

2. $7 + 4 =$ _____

3. $6 + 6 =$ _____

4. $5 + 5 =$ _____

5. $11 + 1 =$ _____

6. $9 + 3 =$ _____

7. $\begin{array}{r} 5 \\ + \ 4 \\ \hline \end{array}$

8. $\begin{array}{r} 10 \\ + \ 2 \\ \hline \end{array}$

9. $\begin{array}{r} 3 \\ + \ 7 \\ \hline \end{array}$

10. $\begin{array}{r} 8 \\ + \ 1 \\ \hline \end{array}$

11. $\begin{array}{r} 4 \\ + \ 6 \\ \hline \end{array}$

12. $\begin{array}{r} 5 \\ + \ 6 \\ \hline \end{array}$

13. $\begin{array}{r} 9 \\ + \ 2 \\ \hline \end{array}$

14. $\begin{array}{r} 7 \\ + \ 5 \\ \hline \end{array}$

Counting back helps you find the difference.
To count back, start with the greater number.
Count 5 numbers back from 11. The difference is 6.

$$\begin{array}{r} 11 \\ -\ 5 \\ \hline 6 \end{array}$$ 10, 9, 8, 7, 6

0 1 2 3 4 5 6 7 8 9 10 11 12

Count back to find the difference.

1. $11 - 4 =$ _____   2. $12 - 5 =$ _____   3. $11 - 2 =$ _____

4. $12 - 7 =$ _____   5. $9 - 3 =$ _____   6. $10 - 6 =$ _____

7. $\begin{array}{r} 12 \\ -\ 4 \\ \hline \end{array}$ 8. $\begin{array}{r} 11 \\ -\ 6 \\ \hline \end{array}$ 9. $\begin{array}{r} 11 \\ -\ 7 \\ \hline \end{array}$ 10. $\begin{array}{r} 12 \\ -\ 8 \\ \hline \end{array}$

11. $\begin{array}{r} 10 \\ -\ 2 \\ \hline \end{array}$ 12. $\begin{array}{r} 11 \\ -\ 5 \\ \hline \end{array}$ 13. $\begin{array}{r} 12 \\ -\ 6 \\ \hline \end{array}$ 14. $\begin{array}{r} 12 \\ -\ 3 \\ \hline \end{array}$

A number line can help you find a sum.
Count 2 more than 5.

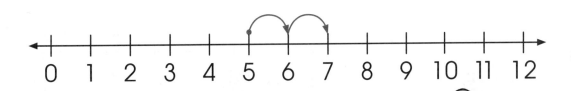

$$\begin{array}{r} 5 \\ + \ 2 \\ \hline 7 \end{array}$$

0 1 2 3 4 5 6 7 8 9 10 11 12

Use the number line to find the sum.

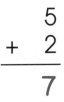

1. $\begin{array}{r} 7 \\ + \ 2 \\ \hline \end{array}$

2. $\begin{array}{r} 5 \\ + \ 5 \\ \hline \end{array}$

3. $\begin{array}{r} 4 \\ + \ 4 \\ \hline \end{array}$

4. $\begin{array}{r} 7 \\ + \ 4 \\ \hline \end{array}$

5. $\begin{array}{r} 8 \\ + \ 4 \\ \hline \end{array}$

6. $\begin{array}{r} 9 \\ + \ 2 \\ \hline \end{array}$

7. $\begin{array}{r} 4 \\ + \ 3 \\ \hline \end{array}$

8. $\begin{array}{r} 6 \\ + \ 2 \\ \hline \end{array}$

9. $\begin{array}{r} 7 \\ + \ 5 \\ \hline \end{array}$

10. $\begin{array}{r} 6 \\ + \ 3 \\ \hline \end{array}$

11. $\begin{array}{r} 8 \\ + \ 2 \\ \hline \end{array}$

12. $\begin{array}{r} 9 \\ + \ 3 \\ \hline \end{array}$

13. $\begin{array}{r} 5 \\ + \ 3 \\ \hline \end{array}$

14. $\begin{array}{r} 4 \\ + \ 5 \\ \hline \end{array}$

15. $\begin{array}{r} 6 \\ + \ 4 \\ \hline \end{array}$

16. $\begin{array}{r} 3 \\ + \ 8 \\ \hline \end{array}$

A number line can help you find a difference.
Count 3 less than 8.

$$\begin{array}{r} 8 \\ -\ 3 \\ \hline 5 \end{array}$$

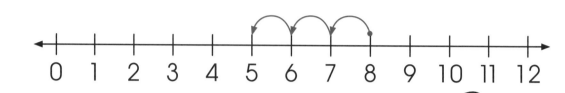

0 1 2 3 4 5 6 7 8 9 10 11 12

Use the number line to find the difference.

1. $\begin{array}{r} 11 \\ -\ 4 \\ \hline \end{array}$
2. $\begin{array}{r} 12 \\ -\ 7 \\ \hline \end{array}$
3. $\begin{array}{r} 8 \\ -\ 3 \\ \hline \end{array}$
4. $\begin{array}{r} 9 \\ -\ 5 \\ \hline \end{array}$

5. $\begin{array}{r} 7 \\ -\ 4 \\ \hline \end{array}$
6. $\begin{array}{r} 9 \\ -\ 4 \\ \hline \end{array}$
7. $\begin{array}{r} 10 \\ -\ 2 \\ \hline \end{array}$
8. $\begin{array}{r} 8 \\ -\ 5 \\ \hline \end{array}$

9. $\begin{array}{r} 9 \\ -\ 6 \\ \hline \end{array}$
10. $\begin{array}{r} 6 \\ -\ 5 \\ \hline \end{array}$
11. $\begin{array}{r} 12 \\ -\ 5 \\ \hline \end{array}$
12. $\begin{array}{r} 10 \\ -\ 4 \\ \hline \end{array}$

13. $\begin{array}{r} 12 \\ -\ 8 \\ \hline \end{array}$
14. $\begin{array}{r} 11 \\ -\ 2 \\ \hline \end{array}$
15. $\begin{array}{r} 9 \\ -\ 8 \\ \hline \end{array}$
16. $\begin{array}{r} 11 \\ -\ 6 \\ \hline \end{array}$

Add or subtract to find the sum or difference.

1. $\begin{array}{r} 8 \\ -\ 3 \\ \hline \end{array}$

2. $\begin{array}{r} 11 \\ -\ 3 \\ \hline \end{array}$

3. $\begin{array}{r} 9 \\ +\ 2 \\ \hline \end{array}$

4. $\begin{array}{r} 10 \\ -\ 4 \\ \hline \end{array}$

5. $\begin{array}{r} 6 \\ +\ 3 \\ \hline \end{array}$

6. $\begin{array}{r} 12 \\ -\ 3 \\ \hline \end{array}$

7. $\begin{array}{r} 6 \\ +\ 4 \\ \hline \end{array}$

8. $\begin{array}{r} 7 \\ +\ 5 \\ \hline \end{array}$

9. $\begin{array}{r} 11 \\ -\ 5 \\ \hline \end{array}$

10. $\begin{array}{r} 9 \\ -\ 6 \\ \hline \end{array}$

11. $\begin{array}{r} 5 \\ +\ 5 \\ \hline \end{array}$

12. $\begin{array}{r} 12 \\ -\ 7 \\ \hline \end{array}$

13. $\begin{array}{r} 8 \\ +\ 2 \\ \hline \end{array}$

14. $\begin{array}{r} 10 \\ -\ 5 \\ \hline \end{array}$

15. $\begin{array}{r} 9 \\ +\ 3 \\ \hline \end{array}$

16. $\begin{array}{r} 12 \\ -\ 5 \\ \hline \end{array}$

Write + or − to make the number sentences true.
The first one is done for you.

1. $9 \boxed{-} 5 = 4$

2. $10 \boxed{} 4 = 6$

3. $6 \boxed{} 6 = 12$

4. $6 \boxed{} 2 = 4$

5. $8 \boxed{} 4 = 12$

6. $7 \boxed{} 4 = 3$

7. $6 \boxed{} 4 = 2$

8. $5 \boxed{} 5 = 10$

9. $4 \boxed{} 6 = 10$

10. $12 \boxed{} 5 = 7$

11. $8 \boxed{} 2 = 10$

12. $11 \boxed{} 9 = 2$

13. $5 \boxed{} 6 = 11$

14. $8 \boxed{} 5 = 3$

15. $6 \boxed{} 3 = 9$

PLANE FIGURES

Draw lines from the objects to the matching figures.
The first one is done for you.

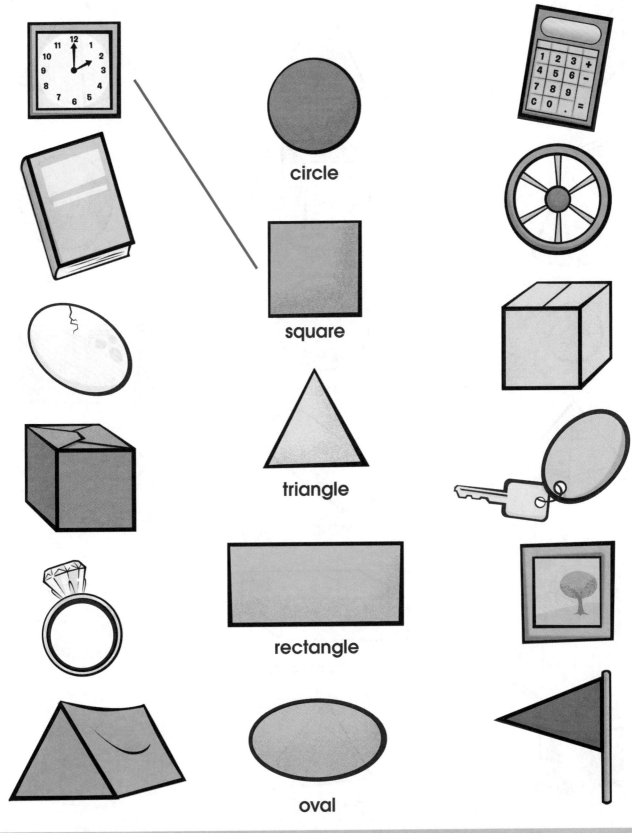

circle

square

triangle

rectangle

oval

SPACE FIGURES

Draw lines from the objects to the matching figures.
The first one is done for you.

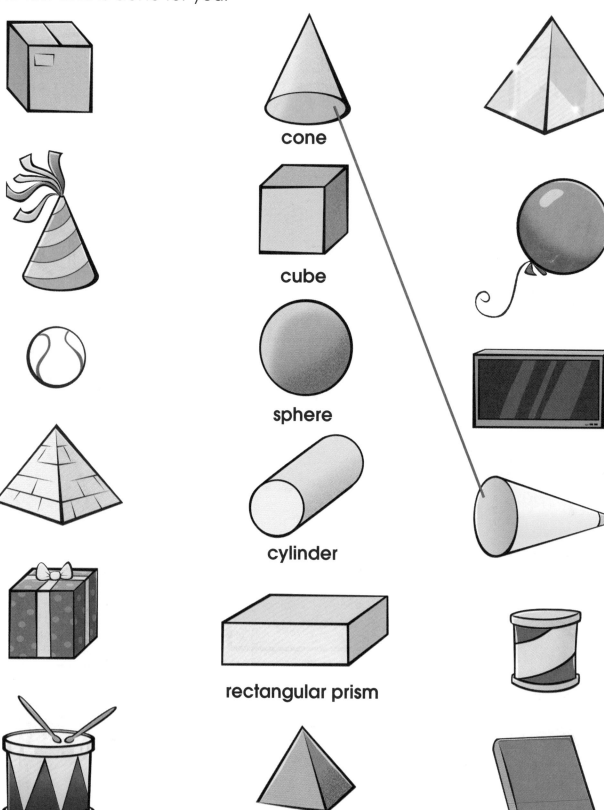

cone

cube

sphere

cylinder

rectangular prism

pyramid

Circle the shape that fits the outline.

1.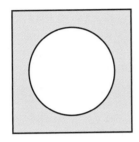

2.

3.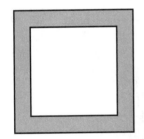

4.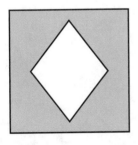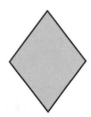

5.

How many are there? Write the number of tens and ones.
The first one is done for you.

1.   __1__ **ten** __10__
ten

2.   ____ **tens** ____
twenty

3.   ____ **tens** ____
thirty

4.   ____ **tens** ____
forty

5. 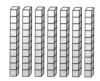 ____ **tens** ____
fifty

6.   ____ **tens** ____
sixty

7. 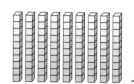 ____ **tens** ____
seventy

8. 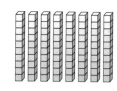 ____ **tens** ____
eighty

9.  ____ **tens** ____
ninety

Write the missing numbers.

10. 10 20 ____ 40 50 ____ 70 80 90 100

11. 10 ____ ____ 40 ____ 60 70 ____ 90 ____

ten __1__ ones __2__   How many s? __12__

Circle groups of ten. Write the number of tens and ones.
Then write how many there are in all.

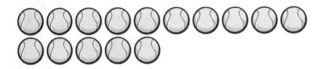

1. ten _____ ones _____

   How many 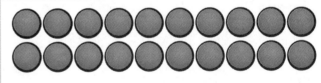s? _____

2. tens _____ ones _____

   How many s? _____

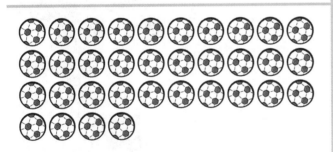

3. tens _____ ones _____

   How many s? _____

4. tens _____ ones _____

   How many s? _____

5. ten _____ ones _____

   How many s? _____

6. ten _____ ones _____

   How many s? _____

Read the numbers.
Write how many tens and how many ones there are.
The first one is done for you.

	tens	ones
1. 65	6	5

	tens	ones
2. 28	___	___

	tens	ones
3. 54	___	___

	tens	ones
4. 66	___	___

	tens	ones
5. 40	___	___

	tens	ones
6. 34	___	___

	tens	one
7. 81	___	___

	ten	ones
8. 17	___	___

	tens	ones
9. 30	___	___

	tens	one
10. 71	___	___

	ten	ones
11. 19	___	___

	tens	ones
12. 25	___	___

GREATER THAN AND LESS THAN

Greater means more than.
Less means not as many.

Circle the number that is greater.
The first one is done for you.

1. 13　(31)

2. 35　27

3. 50　48

4. 43　34

5. 10　15

6. 25　31

7. 18　10

8. 21　19

9. 23　14

Circle the number that is less.
The first one is done for you.

10. (44)　54

11. 18　13

12. 81　18

13. 78　82

14. 25　31

15. 23　36

16. 20　30

17. 62　59

18. 55　48

Write the number that comes **before**.

1. _____ 45   2. _____ 27   3. _____ 24   4. _____ 33

5. _____ 81   6. _____ 30   7. _____ 18   8. _____ 67

Write the number that comes **between**.

9. 91 _____ 93   10. 53 _____ 55   11. 40 _____ 42

12. 24 _____ 26   13. 17 _____ 19   14. 36 _____ 38

Write the number that comes **after**.

15. 6 _____   16. 47 _____   17. 25 _____   18. 19 _____

19. 92 _____   20. 50 _____   21. 74 _____   22. 11 _____

PENNIES, NICKELS, AND DIMES

front back
penny = 1¢

1¢   2¢   3¢   4¢

To count pennies, count by ones.

front back
nickel = 5¢

5¢   10¢   15¢   20¢

To count nickels, count by fives.

front back
dime = 10¢

10¢   20¢   30¢   40¢

To count dimes, count by tens.

Count the coins. Write each amount.

1.    _____¢

2.    _____¢

3.     _____¢

PENNIES, NICKELS, AND DIMES

How much do the clothes cost?
Count on to find the total amounts.
Write the totals on the price tags.

1.

_____ _____ _____ _____ _____ _____

2.

_____ _____ _____ _____ _____ _____

3.

_____ _____ _____ _____ _____ _____

4.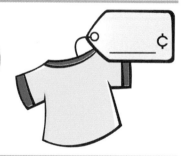

_____ _____ _____ _____ _____ _____

5.

_____ _____ _____ _____ _____ _____

A clock has two hands.
The short hand shows the **hours**.
The long hand shows the **minutes**.

minute hand

hour hand

_____2_____ o'clock

__2__ : __00__

When the long hand points to the 12, we say o'clock.
To which hour does the short hand point?

Write the time.

1. _____ o'clock

_____ : _____

2. _____ o'clock

_____ : _____

3. _____ o'clock

_____ : _____

4. _____ o'clock

_____ : _____

5. _____ o'clock

_____ : _____

6. _____ o'clock

_____ : _____

When the minute hand points to the 6, it is half past the hour. The hour hand is halfway between the current and next hour.

Half past __2__

__2__ : __30__

Write the time.

1. Half past _____

_____ : _____

2. Half past _____

_____ : _____

3. Half past _____

_____ : _____

4. Half past _____

_____ : _____

5. Half past _____

_____ : _____

6. Half past _____

_____ : _____

TIME: QUARTER PAST THE HOUR

When the minute hand points to the 3, it is a quarter past the hour. The hour hand is a little past the hour.

Quarter past ___2___

__2__ : __15__

Write the time.

1. Quarter past _____

____ : ____

2. Quarter past _____

____ : ____

3. Quarter past _____

____ : ____

4. Quarter past _____

____ : ____

5. Quarter past _____

____ : ____

6. Quarter past _____

____ : ____

When the minute hand points to the 9, it is a quarter to the next hour. The hour hand is closer to the next hour.

Quarter to __3__

__2__ : __45__

Write the time.

1. Quarter to _____

____ : ____

2. Quarter to _____

____ : ____

3. Quarter to _____

____ : ____

4. Quarter to _____

____ : ____

5. Quarter to _____

____ : ____

6. Quarter to _____

____ : ____

This shape has two equal parts.
Each part is $\frac{1}{2}$ or one-half of the whole.

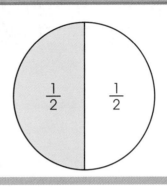

Find the shapes that show one-half.
Write $\frac{1}{2}$ in each part.

1.

2.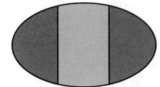

3.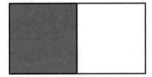

4.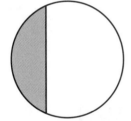

5.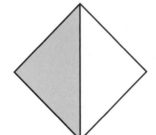

6.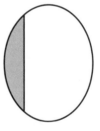

Color $\frac{1}{2}$ of each shape.

7.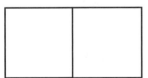

8.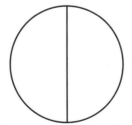

9.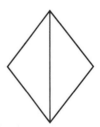

10.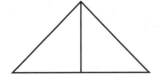

11.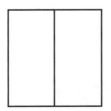

12.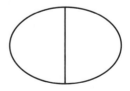

A **fraction** names a part of a whole.
The bottom of a fraction tells how many parts there are in all.

 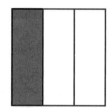 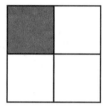

1 of 2 equal parts is $\frac{1}{2}$.   1 of 3 equal parts is $\frac{1}{3}$.   1 of 4 equal parts is $\frac{1}{4}$.

Count the parts of each shape. Write the number in the box to make a fraction. The first one is done for you.

1. 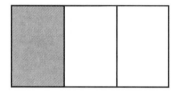 $\dfrac{1}{\boxed{3}}$

2. 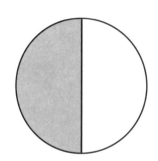 $\dfrac{1}{\square}$

3. 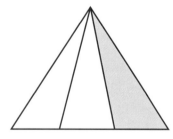 $\dfrac{1}{\square}$

4. 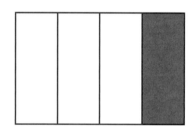 $\dfrac{1}{\square}$

5. 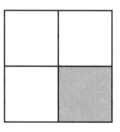 $\dfrac{1}{\square}$

6. 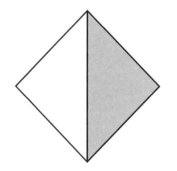 $\dfrac{1}{\square}$

A **fraction** can also name a part of a group.

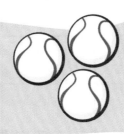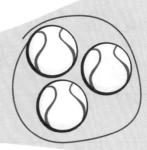

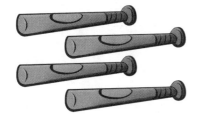

1 of 3 equal parts is $\frac{1}{3}$.

Circle the objects to show each fraction.

1. $\frac{1}{4}$

2. $\frac{1}{2}$

3. $\frac{1}{3}$

4. $\frac{1}{2}$

5. $\frac{1}{4}$

6. $\frac{1}{3}$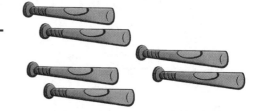

7. $\frac{1}{2}$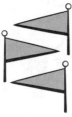

8. $\frac{1}{4}$

Number of Pets

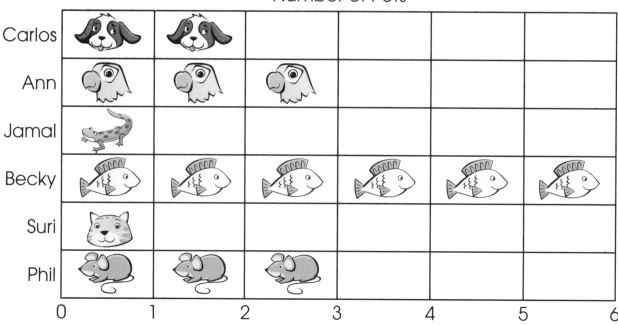

Use the picture graph to answer the questions.
How many pets does each child have?

1. Carlos _____   **2.** Becky _____   **3.** Ann _____

4. Suri _____   **5.** Jamal _____   **6.** Phil _____

7. How many pets do Carlos and Phil have in all?

_____ ☐ _____ = _____

8. Becky has more pets than Ann.
How many more pets does Becky have?

_____ ☐ _____ = _____

ADDING THREE ADDENDS

An **addend** is a number in an addition problem.
Follow these steps to add three addends:

1. Add two of the numbers. Look for a double or numbers with a sum of 10 to make it easier. $3 + 3 = 6$
2. Add the sum to the third number. $6 + 4 = 10$
3. Write the sum. $3 + 3 + 4 = 10$

$$\begin{array}{r} 3 \\ 3 \\ + \ 4 \\ \hline 10 \end{array}$$

Add.

1. $\begin{array}{r} 3 \\ 2 \\ + \ 5 \\ \hline \end{array}$
2. $\begin{array}{r} 1 \\ 2 \\ + \ 8 \\ \hline \end{array}$
3. $\begin{array}{r} 3 \\ 1 \\ + \ 7 \\ \hline \end{array}$
4. $\begin{array}{r} 5 \\ 5 \\ + \ 2 \\ \hline \end{array}$

5. $\begin{array}{r} 6 \\ 2 \\ + \ 2 \\ \hline \end{array}$
6. $\begin{array}{r} 4 \\ 4 \\ + \ 4 \\ \hline \end{array}$
7. $\begin{array}{r} 2 \\ 6 \\ + \ 3 \\ \hline \end{array}$
8. $\begin{array}{r} 2 \\ 4 \\ + \ 5 \\ \hline \end{array}$

9. $\begin{array}{r} 4 \\ 7 \\ + \ 1 \\ \hline \end{array}$
10. $\begin{array}{r} 1 \\ 8 \\ + \ 3 \\ \hline \end{array}$
11. $\begin{array}{r} 4 \\ 4 \\ + \ 2 \\ \hline \end{array}$
12. $\begin{array}{r} 9 \\ 1 \\ + \ 2 \\ \hline \end{array}$

Follow these steps to add tens and ones:

1. Add the ones.

2. Add the tens.

Step 1	Step 2
tens ones	tens ones
24	24
+ 13	+ 13
7	37

Add to find the sum.

1.
```
   27
+  60
```

2.
```
   25
+   3
```

3.
```
   91
+   6
```

4.
```
   45
+  14
```

5.
```
   44
+  34
```

6.
```
   52
+   6
```

7.
```
   60
+   8
```

8.
```
   83
+   6
```

9.
```
   72
+   1
```

10.
```
   63
+   5
```

11.
```
   13
+   4
```

12.
```
   25
+  22
```

SUBTRACTING TENS AND ONES

Follow these steps to subtract tens and ones:

1. Subtract the ones.

2. Subtract the tens.

Step 1	Step 2
tens ones	tens ones
57	57
− 12	− 12
5	45

Subtract to find the difference.

1.
$$38$$
$$- \ 6$$

2.
$$24$$
$$- \ 3$$

3.
$$57$$
$$- \ 5$$

4.
$$98$$
$$- \ 6$$

5.
$$25$$
$$- \ 2$$

6.
$$49$$
$$- \ 7$$

7.
$$47$$
$$- 15$$

8.
$$65$$
$$- 22$$

9.
$$86$$
$$- 26$$

10.
$$96$$
$$- 23$$

11.
$$78$$
$$- 54$$

12.
$$48$$
$$- 34$$

RACE TO THE MONKEYS

Take turns giving the answer to every other problem. The player who has the most correct answers wins.

3 tens + 7 ones = _____

Start

$$\begin{array}{r} 3 \\ +4 \\ \hline \end{array}$$

$$\begin{array}{r} 6 \\ -3 \\ \hline \end{array}$$

$$\begin{array}{r} 8 \\ +2 \\ \hline \end{array}$$

$$\begin{array}{r} 17 \\ -15 \\ \hline \end{array}$$

$$\begin{array}{r} 9 \\ +3 \\ \hline \end{array}$$

$$\begin{array}{r} 36 \\ -24 \\ \hline \end{array}$$

$$13 + 6 = \_\_\_$$

$$\begin{array}{r} 16 \\ +10 \\ \hline \end{array}$$

$$\begin{array}{r} 19 \\ -\square \\ \hline 16 \end{array}$$

$$\begin{array}{r} 8 \\ +4 \\ \hline \end{array}$$

$$\begin{array}{r} 12 \\ -3 \\ \hline \end{array}$$

$$\begin{array}{r} 19 \\ -12 \\ \hline \end{array}$$

$$\begin{array}{r} 6 \\ +\square \\ \hline 12 \end{array}$$

$$\begin{array}{r} 12 \\ -7 \\ \hline \end{array}$$

$$\begin{array}{r} 11 \\ +25 \\ \hline \end{array}$$

$$\begin{array}{r} 18 \\ +11 \\ \hline \end{array}$$

$$\begin{array}{r} 12 \\ -\square \\ \hline 8 \end{array}$$

$$\begin{array}{r} 10 \\ -3 \\ \hline \end{array}$$

6 tens + 4 ones = _____

$$\begin{array}{r} 10 \\ +8 \\ \hline \end{array}$$

$$\begin{array}{r} 15 \\ -\square \\ \hline 10 \end{array}$$

$$\begin{array}{r} 22 \\ -11 \\ \hline \end{array}$$

$$\begin{array}{r} 23 \\ -\square \\ \hline 10 \end{array}$$

$$\begin{array}{r} 11 \\ -7 \\ \hline \end{array}$$

$$\begin{array}{r} 20 \\ +10 \\ \hline \end{array}$$

$$\begin{array}{r} 18 \\ +11 \\ \hline \end{array}$$

$$\begin{array}{r} 11 \\ -\square \\ \hline 7 \end{array}$$

$$\begin{array}{r} 6 \\ +\square \\ \hline 14 \end{array}$$

$$\begin{array}{r} 10 \\ +\square \\ \hline 12 \end{array}$$

$$\begin{array}{r} 32 \\ -\square \\ \hline 20 \end{array}$$

Finish

ANSWER KEY

Page 2
1. dog
2. cat
3. fish
4. bird

Page 3
1. fan, lamp
2. apple, bat
3. ant, ham
4. map, cat

Page 4
1. egg, tent
2. web, bed
3. net, jet
4. ten, nest

Page 5
1. bib, wig
2. ship, six
3. fish, mittens
4. pig, pin

Page 6
1. fox, clock
2. doll, lock
3. box, rocket
4. socks, mop

Page 7
1. sun, rug
2. cup, bus
3. gum, cupcake
4. duck, tub

Page 8

	¹h	²s	o	c	k
	a	u			
³t	e	n			
	g				
⁵p	i	g			

Page 9
1. ten 2. cat 3. pig
4. bus 5. doll 6. fan
7. fish 8. nest 9. duck

Page 10
1. snail
2. cake
3. rain
4. day
5. gray, gate

Page 11
1. three
2. tree
3. sheep
4. leaf
5. he, me

Page 12
1. bike
2. nine
3. ice
4. right
5. tight, tie

Page 13
1. goat
2. rope
3. boat
4. rose
5. nose, note

Page 14
1. tube
2. glue
3. huge
4. cute
5. few, new

Page 15

¹r	a	²k	e			³b
		i				e
⁴t	u	⁵b	e		
		e			o	e
					n	
⁶s	l	i	d	e		

Page 16

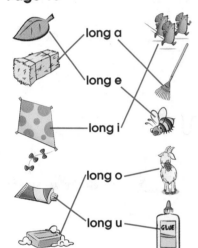

long a
long e
long i
long o
long u

Page 17

4   1   3
5   6   2

Page 18
1. <u>o</u>ur dog is hungry.
2. <u>d</u>ad brings food.
3. <u>s</u>kip eats quickly.
4. <u>f</u>ood goes on the floor.
5. <u>d</u>ogs are messy.
6. <u>n</u>ow I need to clean up.
7. Answers will vary.

Page 19
1. <u>is</u> Mother home?
2. <u>where</u> did she go?
3. <u>when</u> will she be back?
4. <u>who</u> baked the cookies?
5. <u>they</u> are good.
6. <u>may</u> I have another one?
7. Answers will vary.

Page 20
1. Dad
2. farmer
3. cows
4. dog
5. chicken

Page 21

Places	Things
zoo	book
house	pizza
town	bike

Answers will vary. Make sure words name a place or a thing.

Page 22
1. dogs
2. spots
3. ears
4. cats
5. bones

Page 23
1. play
2. hits
3. flies
4. runs
5. catch

Page 24
1. plants
2. grows
3. pulls
4. waters
5. eats

Page 25
1. hot
2. loud
3. cold
4. soft
5. wet

Page 26
1. big
2. three
3. striped
4. black
5. little
6. four
7. Answers will vary. Make sure describing word is underlined.

Page 27
1. don't
2. aren't
3. haven't
4. Let's
5. won't

Page 28
1. 4   2. 2
3. 4   4. 4
5. 5   6. 3

Page 29
1. 2   2. 2
3. 3   4. 1
5. 1   6. 2

Page 30
1. 5   2. 5   3. 8
4. 7   5. 8   6. 7
7. 7   8. 8   9. 8
10. 5   11. 4   12. 4

Page 31

1. 1	2. 4	3. 2
4. 1	5. 4	6. 2
7. 7	8. 1	9. 2
10. 0	11. 6	12. 4

Page 32

1. 7	2. 8	3. 8	4. 6
5. 7	6. 8	7. 7	8. 6
9. 1	10. 0	11. 6	12. 2
13. 3	14. 2	15. 2	16. 3

Page 33

1. 12	2. 11	3. 12	
4. 10	5. 12	6. 12	
7. 9	8. 12	9. 10	10. 9
11. 10	12. 11	13. 11	14. 12

Page 34

1. 7	2. 7	3. 9	
4. 5	5. 6	6. 4	
7. 8	8. 5	9. 4	10. 4
11. 8	12. 6	13. 6	14. 9

Page 35

1. 9	2. 10	3. 8	4. 11
5. 12	6. 11	7. 7	8. 8
9. 12	10. 9	11. 10	12. 12
13. 8	14. 9	15. 10	16. 11

Page 36

1. 7	2. 5	3. 5	4. 4
5. 3	6. 5	7. 8	8. 3
9. 3	10. 1	11. 7	12. 6
13. 4	14. 9	15. 1	16. 5

Page 37

1. 5	2. 8	3. 11	4. 6
5. 9	6. 9	7. 10	8. 12
9. 6	10. 3	11. 10	12. 5
13. 10	14. 5	15. 12	16. 7

Page 38

1. –	2. –	3. +
4. –	5. +	6. –
7. –	8. +	9. +
10. –	11. +	12. –
13. +	14. –	15. +

Page 39

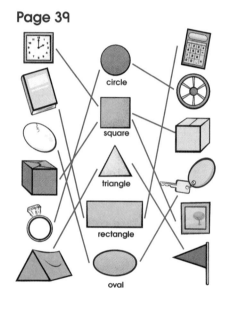

circle, square, triangle, rectangle, oval

Page 40

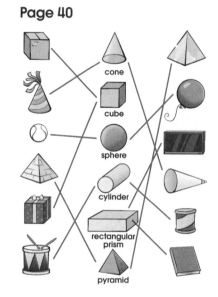

cone, cube, sphere, cylinder, rectangular prism, pyramid

Page 41

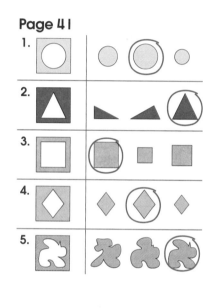

1.
2.
3.
4.
5.

Page 42

1. 1 ten 10	2. 2 tens 20	
3. 3 tens 30	4. 4 tens 40	
5. 5 tens 50	6. 6 tens 60	
7. 7 tens 70	8. 8 tens 80	
9. 9 tens 90		

10. 10, 20, **30**, 40, 50, **60**, 70, 80, 90, 100
11. 10, **20**, **30**, 40, **50**, 60, 70, **80**, 90, **100**

Page 43

1. ten 1 ones 5 15	2. tens 2 ones 2 22
3. tens 3 ones 4 34	4. tens 2 ones 0 20
5. ten 1 ones 7 17	6. ten 1 ones 8 18

Page 44

	tens	ones		tens	ones
1.	6	5	2.	2	8
3.	5	4	4.	6	6
5.	4	0	6.	3	4
7.	8	1	8.	1	7
9.	3	0	10.	7	1
11.	1	9	12.	2	5

Page 45

1. 31	2. 35	3. 50
4. 43	5. 15	6. 31
7. 18	8. 21	9. 23
10. 44	11. 13	12. 18
13. 78	14. 25	15. 23
16. 20	17. 59	18. 48

Page 46

1. 44	2. 26	3. 23	4. 32
5. 80	6. 29	7. 17	8. 66
9. 92	10. 54	11. 41	
12. 25	13. 18	14. 37	
15. 7	16. 48	17. 26	18. 20
19. 93	20. 51	21. 75	22. 12

Page 47
1. 6¢
2. 30¢
3. 80¢

Page 48
1. 10¢, 20¢, 25¢, 26¢, 27¢, 28¢; 28¢
2. 10¢, 20¢, 25¢, 30¢, 31¢, 32¢; 32¢
3. 5¢, 10¢, 15¢, 20¢, 25¢, 26¢; 26¢
4. 5¢, 10¢, 11¢, 12¢, 13¢, 14; 14¢
5. 10¢, 15¢, 20¢, 21¢, 22¢, 23¢; 23¢

Page 49
1. 7 o'clock
   7:00
2. 1 o'clock
   1:00
3. 11 o'clock
   11:00
4. 3 o'clock
   3:00
5. 5 o'clock
   5:00
6. 12 o'clock
   12:00

Page 50
1. Half past 10
   10:30
2. Half past 4
   4:30
3. Half past 9
   9:30
4. Half past 3
   3:30
5. Half past 8
   8:30
6. Half past 6
   6:30

Page 51
1. Quarter past 6
   6:15
2. Quarter past 8
   8:15
3. Quarter past 1
   1:15
4. Quarter past 12
   12:15
5. Quarter past 10
   10:15
6. Quarter past 7
   7:15

Page 52
1. Quarter to 4
   3:45
2. Quarter to 9
   8:45
3. Quarter to 1
   12:45
4. Quarter to 7
   6:45
5. Quarter to 2
   1:45
6. Quarter to 10
   9:45

Page 53
1.
2.
3.
4.
5.
6.
7.
8.
9.
10.
11.
12.

Section colored can vary.

Page 54
1.  $\frac{1}{3}$
2.  $\frac{1}{2}$
3. $\frac{1}{3}$
4. 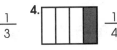 $\frac{1}{4}$
5. $\frac{1}{4}$
6. $\frac{1}{2}$

Page 55
1. $\frac{1}{4}$
2. $\frac{1}{2}$
3. $\frac{1}{3}$
4. $\frac{1}{2}$
5. $\frac{1}{4}$
6. $\frac{1}{3}$
7. $\frac{1}{2}$
8. $\frac{1}{4}$

Objects circled can vary.

Page 56
1. 2 2. 6 3. 3
4. 1 5. 1 6. 3
7. 2 + 3 = 5
8. 6 − 3 = 3

Page 57
1. 10 2. 11 3. 11 4. 12
5. 10 6. 12 7. 11 8. 11
9. 12 10. 12 11. 10 12. 12

Page 58
1. 87 2. 28 3. 97 4. 59
5. 78 6. 58 7. 68 8. 89
9. 73 10. 68 11. 17 12. 47

Page 59
1. 32 2. 21 3. 52 4. 92
5. 23 6. 42 7. 32 8. 43
9. 60 10. 73 11. 24 12. 14

Page 60

Start
$\begin{array}{r}3\\+4\\\hline7\end{array}$
$\begin{array}{r}6\\-3\\\hline3\end{array}$
$\begin{array}{r}8\\+2\\\hline10\end{array}$
$\begin{array}{r}17\\-15\\\hline2\end{array}$
$\begin{array}{r}9\\+3\\\hline12\end{array}$
$\begin{array}{r}36\\-24\\\hline12\end{array}$
13 + 6 = 19

$\begin{array}{r}16\\+10\\\hline26\end{array}$	$\begin{array}{r}12\\-7\\\hline5\end{array}$	$\begin{array}{r}11\\+25\\\hline36\end{array}$
$\begin{array}{r}19\\-3\\\hline16\end{array}$		$\begin{array}{r}18\\+11\\\hline29\end{array}$
$\begin{array}{r}8\\+4\\\hline12\end{array}$		$\begin{array}{r}12\\-4\\\hline8\end{array}$
$\begin{array}{r}12\\-3\\\hline9\end{array}$		$\begin{array}{r}10\\-3\\\hline7\end{array}$
$\begin{array}{r}19\\-12\\\hline7\end{array}$		
$\begin{array}{r}6\\+6\\\hline12\end{array}$		

3 tens + 7 ones = 37

$\begin{array}{r}10\\+8\\\hline18\end{array}$	$\begin{array}{r}18\\+11\\\hline29\end{array}$
$\begin{array}{r}15\\-5\\\hline10\end{array}$	$\begin{array}{r}11\\-4\\\hline7\end{array}$
$\begin{array}{r}22\\-11\\\hline11\end{array}$	$\begin{array}{r}6\\+8\\\hline14\end{array}$
$\begin{array}{r}23\\-10\\\hline13\end{array}$	$\begin{array}{r}10\\+2\\\hline12\end{array}$
$\begin{array}{r}11\\-7\\\hline4\end{array}$	$\begin{array}{r}32\\-12\\\hline20\end{array}$
$\begin{array}{r}20\\+10\\\hline30\end{array}$	Finish

6 tens + 4 ones = 64

AWARD

Great Job!

_____

Name

has completed First Grade Basics
from School Zone Publishing Company.